The IEA Health and Welfare Unit

Religion and Liberty Series No. 1

Christian Capitalism
or
Christian Socialism?

The IEA Health and Welfare Unit

Religion and Liberty Series No. 1

Christian Capitalism
or
Christian Socialism?

Michael Novak

Ronald Preston

IEA Health and Welfare Unit
London, 1994

First published in April 1994
by
The IEA Health and Welfare Unit
2 Lord North St
London SW1P 3LB

ISBN 0-255 36352-4

Typeset by the IEA Health and Welfare Unit
in Palatino 11 on 12 point
Printed in Great Britain by
Goron Pro-Print Co. Ltd
Churchill Industrial Estate, Lancing, West Sussex

Contents

Foreword

The case for the practical superiority of socialism over market economies has now all but collapsed. In the words of America's most distinguished Marxist, Robert Heilbroner:

> Less than seventy-five years after it officially began, the contest between capitalism and socialism is over: capitalism has won.[1]

Put simply, capitalist or market economies provide people (including poor people) with a higher standard of living than socialist or planned economies. That is not to say, however, that socialism has no defenders left. Socialism continues to find advocates among certain groups within Western societies, including academics, entertainers and churchmen. They argue for socialism not because it creates more wealth (it clearly does not) but because it is said to be fairer. The case hinges upon concepts of social justice, rather than economic growth.

Capitalism continues to be regarded as a system which promotes greed and selfishness, while socialism claims the moral high ground of generosity and altruism. The allure of these false associations remains strong. For example, the public opinion polls prior to the General Election in 1992 were notoriously inaccurate, predicting a Labour victory up until the close of polling. A post-election enquiry by the opinion pollsters came to the conclusion that Conservative voters had misrepresented their voting intentions, or had refused to answer, because they were embarrassed to admit their support for a party which was seen as promoting wealth creation above 'caring'. Of course they voted Conservative just the same.

The two contributors to this volume, Michael Novak and Ronald Preston, both argue that theories of political economy must have a moral dimension. To support any system from purely selfish motives is undesirable for the development of the individual as a moral being, and for society as a whole. A political or economic system which lacks a moral or philosophical base is weak and vulnerable, and may be unable to preserve the liberty of its people. Preston cites the example of Hong Kong, which he believes to be trading on the residue of the Confucian family ethic which may eventually expire.

Both Novak and Preston write as Christians, one from the Roman Catholic and one from the Protestant tradition, addressing the rival claims of capitalism and socialism. Novak writes as a former suporter of socialism who became disillusioned with its inability to live up to its promises. Preston cites the influence of a mixture of classical economics and Christian socialism on his intellectual development which has put him politically on the left, whilst remaining sceptical of the claims of the various Christian socialist movements. Both write from backgrounds of wide reading and profound thinking on their subjects, and neither ignores the shortcomings of his preferred system.

They both consider the difficult question of the relationship between the individual and the community which the rival claims of capitalism and socialism present to the Christian conscience. Is capitalism excessively individualistic, at the expense of the wider community? Or is socialism excessively communistic, at the expense of freedom of choice which, alone, allows for the moral growth of the individual through the voluntary excercise of virtue? Should there be a 'trade-off' between the two systems, mixing the market's capacity for creating wealth with a role for the state in redistributing it?

These are serious questions which the churches need to address. It is open to debate whether or not modern British (and Western) society is Christian or not. It may perhaps be more accurately described as post-Christian. The fact remains that its institutions and moral and legal codes reflect the assumptions of the Judeao-Christian tradition which is its heritage.

The IEA Health and Welfare Unit is proud to publish *Christian Capitalism or Christian Socialism?* as the first title in the *Religion and Liberty* series. Whilst the Institute of Economic Affairs holds no corporate view on any subject, it is hoped that the publication of considered essays by two leading thinkers on the subject will assist in determining the respective moral claims of the two main political philosophies of the modern world.

Robert Whelan

Notes

1   Heilbroner, R., *The New Yorker*, January 1989, p. 98.

The Authors

Professor Ronald Preston read Economics and Economic History at the London School of Economics, where he was a pupil of R.H. Tawney. After working as a layman, he read Theology at Oxford and was ordained in Sheffield Diocese. Most of his working life has been spent in Manchester, connected to Manchester Cathedral, as Canon Theologian, and Manchester University, where after being a lecturer in Christian Ethics he became the first Professor of Social and Pastoral Theology.

Professor Preston has contributed to many symposia, the latest being 'Principles of Health Care Ethics'. He has written several books, including *Religion and the Persistence of Capitalism; Church Society in the Late Twentieth Century*, and *Religion and the Ambiguities of Capitalism*; and edited, among others, *Technology and Social Justice*, and *The Coming Penal Crisis*.

Ronald Preston has been associated with the ecumenical movement for many years, especially its Church and Society Unit.

Professor Michael Novak holds the George Frederick Jewett Chair in Religion and Public Policy at the American Enterprise Institute in Washington, D.C. He has written over twenty influential books in the areas of politics, economics and culture, including, *The Spirit of Democratic Capitalism*, 1982, 1991; *Catholic Social Thought and Liberal Institutions*, 1984; *Will It Liberate? Questions about Liberation Theology*, 1986 and *Free Persons and the Common Good*, 1989. He also wrote the text of the influential *New Consensus on Family and Welfare*, 1987. His latest book is *The Catholic Ethic and the Spirit of Capitalism*, 1993.

Professor Novak's writings have appeared in every major Western language, and in Bengali, Korean and Japanese. *The Spirit of Democratic Capitalism* has been reprinted often in Latin America, and was published underground in Poland in 1986. In January 1989 *Forbes Magazine* began running his new column 'The Larger Context'. Since 1993, he has been the Editor of the lay Catholic monthly *Crisis*.

In March 1994 Michael Novak was awarded the Templeton Prize for Progress in Religion.

viii

The Person In Community

Michael Novak

Two mentors have meant more to me than any others: Jacques Maritain, whose *The Person and the Common Good*[1] inspired my own poor attempt at updating the argument in *Free Persons and the Common Good*; and Reinhold Niebuhr, who explained in one of his last books, *Man's Nature and His Communities*,[2] that he had earlier too little appreciated the Jewish and Catholic sense of community, and too uncritically accepted a Protestant emphasis on the individual.

Thus, it surprises me when fairminded critics in Britain see in my work 'excessive individualism'. I would have thought I present a rich Catholic account of community (but not a European account). On the other hand, I must confess to finding British writers in the field of religious social ethics emphasizing community rather more than seems just. In this difference in emphasis, no doubt, some substantive differences are at stake. Regarding substantive differences, I would be happy to press the argument further and, if necessary, to amend my views or otherwise explore the implications of irreducible but exactly located disagreement. (It is not easy to achieve exact disagreement, and so even to get that far would represent a significant mapping of difficult territory.) Yet I cannot help believing that, at least initially, some of the differences spring from the quite different horizons of social experience in Britain and in America.

The social texture of Britain is not, for me, well known terrain, and so in what follows I speak with diffidence. Still, I am quite regularly (and agreeably) surprised by the many expressions of courtesy and deference that I encounter among ordinary people in Britain. A sense of fittingness, status, and open willingness to help seem to be part of the national character, even a nicely inflected sense of hierarchy. A kind of

1

'organic' social sense still makes its presence felt in daily manners, more so than in America, with the possible exception of the American South. There, too, an aristocratic sense of manners and courtesy, chivalry even, are still encountered, along with the kind of social softness one associates with the code of the Christian gentleman. To my mind, this seems like a still living echo of the medieval code of charity deeply rooted in ancient institutions, practices, and manners. I respond to it as 'almost Christian', meaning by that phrase the work of a profoundly Christian culture but marked also by the limitations of its historical period. (I recall Cardinal Newman writing somewhere that the people of Britain may exemplify better than any other the kindliness Christianity sought to infuse into daily intercourse among peoples; and I recall, on reflection, thinking that plausible.)

Possibly, John Wesley's Methodism played an important role in bringing such social sweetness to British manners or at least in keeping it alive into the modern era. Whatever the actual historical roots and determinants of the sensibility I am trying to describe—a sensibility different from what I experience in America—this powerful sense of respect for others deserves to be acknowledged and praised. It is, I think, the ground of social experience that British philosophers and theologians assume, as if it were universal. Yet when British writers describe what is 'natural' or when they give examples from daily life, it is obvious to foreigners that the traits they take for granted are not to be taken for granted in other climes and places. Such terms as 'sympathy', 'fellow feeling', and 'moral sentiments' have here a resonance that one would wish were universal, but are not. Where else in the world are queues so orderly and sweet-tempered? Queuing for a bus in Rome and in London are two quite different experiences. When reading British writers such as Bentham and Mill on 'the individual', one must remind oneself that in their world social rules and social expectations have already been internalized.

Some Autobiographical Reflections

I have always found it useful in trying to understand why a given author places the emphasis where he does to inquire into at least the large outlines of his own personal narrative. Usually, particularly in the field of ethics, we are taught our most important lessons by life itself. My grandfather was a migrant from the mountains of Slovakia to the mountains of Western Pennsylvania, where he went to work as a miner. One of his sons went to work as a steel worker, another as an employee of a large department store, and the third (my father) had to quit school after the sixth grade in order to go to work. Some of my cousins are, still today, local labour union leaders among the men at the mills. Partly to honour my grandfather and them, I devoted one of my books, *The Guns of Lattimer*, to an important incident in the founding of the United Mine Workers.[3]

For most of my conscious life, since the age of 14, I have thought of myself as a Democrat, and on the progressive wing of that party. One of my college-day heroes was Michael Harrington, probably the leading socialist of his generation in America. After having studied for the Roman Catholic priesthood for many years, I went to Harvard for graduate studies, and later accepted positions at Stanford University, the State University of New York at Old Westbury, and finally a tenured distinguished professorship at Syracuse University. During the academic year 1971-72, I took a leave of absence in order to work for the Democratic nominee (whoever it would be) to defeat Richard Nixon. The upshot was that I ended up writing speeches for George McGovern and travelling on the aeroplane with his vice presidential candidate, Sargent Shriver, for the last nine weeks of the campaign as his chief speech writer.

I was, however, becoming more and more disillusioned with the left in American politics, and, indeed, in the world in general. I could not think of a single socialist country that I truly admired and would wish to put forward as a model for the United States. For a long time, I comforted myself that, as an idea, socialism is superior to capitalism, but, as far as its failed experiments go, we just hadn't quite got the hang of it yet in practice. In short, the theory was better, but the practice wasn't yet what we wanted. Then doubt began to creep in. If after so many different experiments the practice kept failing, perhaps, then, something really was wrong with the fundamental idea. I came to think that socialism was based on a false idea. It was based on a false anthropology, and its romance with the centralizing state was a mistake. But then what? What

3

alternative to socialism really is there for a progressive intellectual?

As Hayek has explained in his potent little essay, 'The Intellectuals and Socialism',[4] socialism serves the intellectuals very well by supplying a clear and vivid narrative line for all of human history. Those who love big ideas have in socialism the equivalent of well-defined longitudes and latitudes. Whatever strengthens the central government, the collective, the community, is good; whatever is left to private initiatives and interests is suspect. I'm exaggerating, of course. But the idea was: Society exists first, then the individual. The next step was to hold that the political (and most potent) instrument of society is the state, and to derive from this the practical corollary that one ought to bring as much as possible of economic life under political—that is, state—control. Even when socialism, learning by experience, turned away from the program of nationalizing industries, its proponents (at least in America) always had a knack for launching new government initiatives, and taking away the free space formerly inhabited by civil society and private initiatives.

Increasingly, I could see how progressive programs in America were going wrong. Things I had fought for and contributed to—such as the War on Poverty with its multiplicity of programmes—went badly and even turned sour. I don't mean that there were no successes. The War on Poverty did work rather well for the elderly, especially through the programme of universal health care for the elderly, Medicare. Social Security benefits (America's income programme for the elderly) and other benefits were both enriched and indexed for inflation in a way quite favourable to the elderly. Correspondingly, the condition of those over 65 years of age is in 1993 vastly better than it was in 1963. This was a significant success.

Nonetheless, the damage done to the families of the younger poor as the new welfare programs have taken hold, and to their morale and general condition, has been highly visible and very considerable. There has emerged what never before existed in American society, the urban (so-called) 'underclass'. Morale in urban ghettos seems in some ways worse than in 1963, although the sums of money sloshing around in them are vastly larger than for any generation of the poor in the past. Yet the poor in the past were, on the whole, far more successful in escaping from poverty rather quickly. Indeed, most of the new immigrants coming to America in the almost unprecedented numbers of the 1970s, 1980s, and still today are even now escaping from poverty more quickly than those who have been caught in what the newcomers warn one another against as the 'welfare trap'. By this they mean the Siren call of seemingly free benefits, whose hidden cost is the fear of losing them by finding work; that is, a kind of permanent dependency.

With a team of twenty others, I led a study group to assess what had gone well and what had gone badly in the war on poverty and how we might yet do better. The text put out by this group was called *The New Consensus on Family and Welfare*.[5] Many of the facts that it reported, its way of reporting them, its distinctions and its recommendations have become part of the mainstream of public policy discourse in the U.S., although not yet part of public policy. Candidate Bill Clinton seemed to be drawing on them during his electoral campaign. Clinton ran as though he were more 'neoconservative' than 'liberal' on welfare and foreign policy, although on moral and cultural questions (such as abortion, gay rights, and support for the teachers' unions) he plainly leaned left.

Here a terminological note may prove helpful. In Britain, no clear distinction is drawn between the American 'neoconservatives' and the British 'New Right' (although, to his credit, Samuel Brittan does make it, and well). In the United States, we would call your New Right 'libertarians', including among them such persons as Milton Friedman and other economists and activists of the 'classical liberal' school; their chief centre in Washington is now the Cato Institute and, to a lesser degree, the Heritage Foundation. To such persons, the term 'conservative' suggests sympathies for cultural traditionalism which they do not share. Again, although our libertarians take economic positions close to those of your 'New Right', they worry that the 'New Right' might suggest 'Religious Right', by whom they are rather repelled. Indeed libertarians do not feel as though they are 'new' anything. They claim a long and noble lineage, which in their hands is (they think) more progressive, futuristic, and technically proficient than anything they see around them.

To most leftists, of course, everything to the right is a bit of a blur. Since some of them think that they occupy the one true moral position, beyond which all else is outer darkness, they hardly need to make distinctions to their right. As a result they make many mistakes in identifying arguments that are flying in on them from their right. While this is understandable, it is also an advantage to the right. When leftists return fire to their right they seldom shoot straight.

In the United States, when some thinkers began in the 1970s to become critical of their former leftist positions in an increasingly fundamental way, those who remained on the left gave them the name 'neoconservative'. (In this case, the first one to use that epithet was the highly respected Socialist, Michael Harrington.) It was not a name any of us at first welcomed. In America 'conservatives' had traditionally been thought of as 'the stupid party'. Of course, that's exactly why Michael Harrington chose that particular name. In an irony of history that would have delighted Reinhold Niebuhr, however, that name became an advantage for the tiny band of apostate-leftists who were suddenly linked by an accident of terminology to the 'new conservatives' surrounding Ronald Reagan and Margaret Thatcher. Not that we minded. Most of us had, in fact, supported the election of Ronald Reagan over Jimmy Carter, and cheered the coming to power of Mrs. Thatcher. But we were prodigal sons, come in at the last hour, and we could not blame those conservatives who had toiled in the heat for so long, when in the flush of victory they had to swallow very hard at our being given credit equal to theirs.

Here, I think, narrative history does make a difference. We American neoconservatives had begun as persons of the left. We had a leftwing past, in some cases flamboyantly so. Moreover, we retained some important parts of our basic progressive outlook, even while finding a dynamo different from the state to drive history. We were turning, instead, towards civil society or to what many of us first called 'mediating institutions'. We were still looking for a social theory. We still thought, with Peguy, that *politique* begins in *mystique*. Unlike such conservatives as Russell Kirk, who faulted us for being 'ideological', we believed in visions of the future—no longer constructivist visions in which the state played the role of hero. But visions, nonetheless, of the future.

Those who have the more compelling vision of the future, we still believed, own the moral high ground. We were willing to learn a great deal from authors we had earlier paid far less attention to: from Ferguson, Hutcheson, and Adam Smith; from Edmund Burke, James Madison, and Abraham Lincoln; and from Friedrich Hayek and Ludwig von Mises, as well as Alexis de Tocqueville and Lord Acton.

In addition, there is a religious component to American neoconservativism. Many of us are in reaction against secularism and are, or have become, rather more serious about our Catholic and/or Jewish roots. (Those Protestants who are our allies tend to have been conservatives all along.) Some of us thought of Reinhold Niebuhr as 'the first neoconservative', since a full generation before our own he had slowly but doggedly learned from biblical realism to reject, in turn, pacifism, marxism, socialism, and liberal idealism. Niebuhr had for Winston Churchill, a Conservative, the sort of esteem that we had for Reagan and Thatcher, and for analogous reasons, as one can see in his essays on what he disliked in liberalism and what he admired in conservatism.[6]

Neoconservatives have been few in number, but the arguments they developed have more often than not caught those on the left from flanks on which they were not prepared to fight. Countervolleys on neoconservatives from those on the right who began to call themselves 'palæoconservatives' fell harmlessly to the ground. The number of neoconservatives has, therefore, tended to be systematically overestimated. The truth is that, though few in number, they placed some new arguments on the table, and attacked from new directions and towards new objectives. Above all, they offered the public a more attractive picture of the future than the left did, and the left wasn't used to this. Heretofore, against conservatives, the left had always had a monopoly on ideas about the future. Now they no longer did. In the fields of politics and economics, therefore, the neoconservatives won many arguments, whereas in the fields of culture and the arts, the progressives have continued to dominate the public culture.

That is why the next set of battles shapes up as the 'culture wars'.

Excesses of Community

Those on the left often speak of 'excessive individualism'. By contrast, those of us who have abandoned the left have often been disillusioned by excesses of community. We came to see that the good name of community was often being used as an instrument to enhance the powers of the state, and to make government an ever more dominant factor in individual lives. For more than a hundred years, the movement toward ever bigger government has dominated our world, with vast intellectual and media support.

I don't know how it is in Britain. But in America, a decade in which more and more space is given to the private sector is described as 'a decade of greed'. However, any decade in which more and more emphasis is given to government programmes is described as 'a decade of idealism'. The activities of the state are idealized; the activities of private citizens are regarded with suspicion. Surely, this is an inversion of reality. Reinhold Niebuhr called one of his early books (from his most socialist, indeed, almost communist period) *Moral Man and Immoral Society*.[7] Chastened, he later said that he probably should have called it 'Not So Moral Man and His Even Less Moral Communities.'

Neoconservatives have retained a strong sense of community—or, rather, of many communities: their own historical religious communities; their families and heritages; and the free society they have inherited, with all its vibrant and vigorous associations, organizations, and other expressions of self-government. They are not against the state. They know, with Jefferson, that 'to secure these rights, governments are instituted among men'. They respect government, but they do not want to see it enlarged. They do not want to see it engorge itself by swallowing up the liberties of its citizens. They have come to believe that the state is one of the greatest over-promisers and under-achievers of our century. Its enlarged size and its unappeasable appetite for public funds have become a threat to the practical survival of democracy in the twenty-first century.

In his very helpful book, *The Ambiguities of Capitalism*,[8] for example, Ronald Preston mentions at least twice his annoyance with the phrase 'the taxpayers' money', when it is used in the context of trying to limit both taxation and public spending.

What he finds annoying about this expression, he explains, is that no taxpayer earns his income through his private efforts alone. On the contrary, the efforts of each of us depend upon many contributions from others, including the contributions of government itself through infrastructure, order, and many other common goods. In this sense, what the taxpayer earns, he owes in large part to others.

There is a certain truth in this. But experience also shows that a society which looks at things that way, and insists on that point, is likely to become a sluggish and declining society. The only real source of human creativity, invention, discovery, and enterprise is implanted in the individual; it derives from God, and is endowed in every woman and man. Every human person has been made in the Creator's own image. That is where the spark of creativity is born. You can emphasize the social contribution, if you wish, and diminish the role of the individual. In doing so, you are quite likely to dampen the tinder of originality and inventiveness.

I want to repeat: the cause of the wealth of nations is the human capacity to invent, discover, and create. Yet crucial to the activation of this capacity is social and institutional support. Humans must learn to see the institutional system of wealth-creation as a whole; they must help to establish institutions appropriate to it; they must attend to experience, so as to grasp connections between causes and results; they must rise to a complex social vision of the requirements of the free society in all their ramifications and relationships. Before individuals can become fully and personally creative, they must first get the social *system* right.

Not every social system serves liberty. Most human systems that have appeared in history have repressed the right of personal economic initiative endowed by God in every woman and man. Nonetheless, always beyond where we are now, there is a system of natural liberty that humans must ardently seek—through trial and error, through attentiveness, and with longing. It is a great gift and great grace to have come through experiment to a closer approximation of the system most suited to human creativity.

More concretely, by studying the historical record, I have come to believe that it better serves the common good for

9

society or, rather, for each of us to encourage one another to be creative, inventive, and enterprising, and to stress the originality and initiative of which each of us is capable, by the grace of God. Each of us has a distinctive contribution to make, one that can be made by no other. It is part of a very real adventure of life for each of us to find that spark of originality and uniqueness that the Creator placed in us, and to strike from it the fires that no other individual can bring into the world. A society that encourages the full development of this side of our nature will, experience shows, do far more to enrich the common good than a society that does not.

Imagine that all nations are running a race, such as the race to which St. Paul compared the race for salvation. (In this imagined case, the stakes are nothing like so large.) There are many possible constitutions of society. We should evaluate societies by their fruits. Every social arrangement implies tradeoffs. Constitute society this way, and certain fruits may become unattainable, but others more frequent. Constitute society that way, and a different pattern emerges. If you design the society badly, its institutions are likely to frustrate or to repress the creativity of its individuals. If you place an excess of emphasis on society, you are likely to get a society of greater uniformity but of rather less sparkle, originality, and creativity.

Moreover, the common good of a traditional society composed of obedient and dependent subjects is quite different from the common good of a society composed of free citizens. Contrast the lives of my great grandparents four generations ago in the mountains of Slovakia, living as serfs under a Hungarian count, with our lives today. If you will forgive me an exaggeration for the sake of brevity, they could be good subjects by meeting three obligations: 'Pray, pay, and obey'. The lives of their great grandchildren in a free republic such as ours in the United States (or in a constitutional monarchy such as in Britain) include far more self-determination, room for initiative, need for enterprise and self-reliance, and moral risk.

Again, in a traditional society, it is the task of the rulers to discern the common good for all, to point it out, and to move their subjects toward it. In a free society, in an important sense, the citizens themselves are the sovereigns. They are responsible for their own self-government. The state and the community are constituted to serve the free person, rather than the reverse. Of course, it is quite true that a free person will not develop as fully as a human being can, except in a lively community of inquiry, mutual respect, and friendship with others. Even further, giving one's life for the community is a most noble act. Still, the community also exists for the sake of the person. The community cannot use persons merely as means to its own ends. The most beautiful of God's creatures is the human person, to whom no star in the skies, nor any living creature in the jungles or in the seas is an equal. The person is made in the image of God. *Communio* (being in relation with other persons through self-critical love) enters into the very essence of person, as in the Trinity.

So it is true that the person is fulfilled only in community. It is also true that, as a given of Christian faith, our God is communitarian, Three-in-One, a community of persons. But one should not oppose person and community as though they were contradictories. Each was made for the other. In many contexts, it serves even community better to give stronger emphasis to the emerging person.

In that respect, the span of history during which the individual has had room to breathe, to distinguish himself over against the community, and as often as possible to utter his singular voice in the public square, is a relatively short span of human history. For most of human history, the individual did not emerge from the common crowd. A few great ones did, of course, but not many individuals from among the masses. Only in the modern period did new types of societies develop institutions that treated each citizen as a sovereign, and impose upon each citizen important responsibilities for seizing the initiative and launching enterprises without which the work of the community could not be done. In the demands it makes upon its citizens, a free society is quite different from a traditional society. It calls forth a rather different panoply of virtues.

Traditional lists of virtues never go completely out of date. But to them must today be added many new and distinctively modern virtues. For modern societies are considerably more demanding than ancient or medieval societies. They demand of us, for example, the virtues of enterprise; initiative; civic spiritedness; the habit of voluntary cooperation with others; and all those habits and skills of associating oneself with others for social purposes that go by the name of 'social justice'. They elicit a new sense of responsibility that causes a citizen to look around and see what needs to be done for the common good and then to start doing it, without prompting from others, on his or her own initiative.

Indeed, perhaps this is the point to make a few observations about that very badly used concept, 'social justice'. That term was first used by a Sicilian priest, Taparelli d'Azeglio, in his *Theoretical Essay on Natural Rights Based on Facts*.[9] It is a modern term intended to meet modern necessities. Unfortunately, it was formulated during the period when socialism was rising to its zenith, and thus tempted many partisans of socialism to bend the word toward socialist purposes. They understood 'justice' to mean (preeminently) 'equality', and their inherent drive toward bigger government led them to aim to achieve this through coercive redistribution. Social justice, therefore, became another name for schemes of taxation and regulation by government, in order, so it was said, to equalize the incomes and the circumstances of individuals.

This is a flagrant misuse of the term. First of all, social justice was from the first intended as the name of a virtue. But if the term social justice is applied only to the redistributive state, it does not name a virtue but a particular arrangement of society. Only persons can practice virtues. Only persons can practice social justice. In fact, Pope Leo XIII, who first gave the term canonical use in *Rerum Novarum*,[10] was called 'the Pope of associations', and plainly had in mind as the carrier of social justice, not the state, but the institutions of civil society. For most of its history, in fact, the church fulfilled its mission to care for the poor, the sick, and the needy predominantly through the institutions of civil society, since states were quite weak and sufficiently overburdened by the infrequently achieved tasks of establishing order and the rule of law. (For how difficult this achievement was in pre-modern Britain, which did better than most, see Paul Johnson's *A History of the English People*.)[11] In 1891 Leo XIII was justifiably eager to block the growth of the unlimited modern state. He urged free citizens by the practice of this virtue to associate themselves with one another to accomplish necessary social tasks, sometimes through the state, but more ordinarily through their own associations. It is necessary to keep the state limited and not to feed its appetite. The best way to do this is to encourage citizens to become more active in the exercise of the virtue aptly described as *social* justice.

This virtue is called 'social' because both its aim and its method are social: both to improve social conditions and to do so by association with other free citizens. It is called 'justice' because through it individual citizens meet the responsibilities inherent in their status as sovereigns over a free republic, responsible as self-governing citizens for the common good. This virtue came to prominence only in modern times, for only in modern times were institutions developed that placed so many social responsibilities— political, economic, and cultural—on the shoulders of free citizens in new types of societies.

This explanation of social justice, incidentally, turns aside Hayek's rather trenchant critique of the usual sloppy ways in which the term is vulgarly used. It also illuminates how Hayek's own life work, e.g. in founding the Mont Pelerin Society (and many other institutions vitalizing the free society) was itself an example of the practice of social justice. According to his own lights, Hayek worked tirelessly to improve the society in which he found himself, in ways corresponding to the responsibilities inherent in 'the constitution of liberty' and to the common good, as he saw it, of the human race; and he was a genius at getting others to work with him to establish free and self-governing associations for this task.

The Market

I said earlier that the historical fate of the individual depends a great deal on the *design* of the social *system* in which he lives, moves, and has his temporal being. And thus a crucial question arises: What sort of system can possibly maximize personal liberty while encouraging social cooperation, fellow feeling and sympathy, the rule of law, and personal initiative and accountability, while also moving toward the attainment of universal opulence? This last phrase was invented by Adam Smith as the name of his own dream, the liberation of all human beings on earth from the prison of poverty, such as

13

could be seen c. 1770 in Scotland, France, Italy, Africa, the Middle East, India, the wilds of the Americas, and China. There were then about 780 million human beings on earth; most were desperately poor, only thirty million or so lived in regimes that might be called free, a great many were outright slaves or, near to it, penniless serfs, and the average age at death was about 18. In many places—and not only in prisons, dungeons, and in the ranks of the rowers of galleys—the human condition was quite literally 'nasty, brutish, and short'.

In such circumstances, those who could come up with ways of organizing society better would, indeed, be benefactors of humanity and practitioners of social justice in the sense just defined. And in fact, by about 1770, the human race had learned a few important lessons. The best account of these lessons as they were seen at that time has just been published by Jerry Z. Muller, a young intellectual historian in America.[12] Smith, Muller reminds us, became one of the founders of modern social science through being preoccupied with finding a social theory that would give rise to a society without the poverty, oppression, and misery so evident in the world around him.

For Smith, 'natural man is social man'. Further, natural man is endowed with two quite basic social dispositions according to Smith, 'imagination' and 'sympathy'. Imagination allows a man 'to put himself in the position of others and to judge his own conduct accordingly'. Sympathy allows him 'to share the emotions of others and to control his own behaviour in accord with shared social standards'. In judging his feelings and actions by these two standards with as much impartiality as he can muster, the wise man 'almost identifies himself with, he almost becomes, that impartial spectator, and scarce even feels but as that great arbiter of his conduct directs him to feel'. Smith's lifetime quest was to try to imagine, before they yet fully existed, the sorts of social institutions that would make the occurrence of such acts of imagination and sympathy—guided by the impartial spectator—frequent, regular, and relatively easy for free citizens.

In this search, Smith was the beneficiary of a quite subtle and realistic debate among the theologians of his generation, Muller tells us, concerning human weakness and the difficulty of acting always as a Christian ought to act. Human beings often sin against one another even when social circumstances are highly favourable, and all the more so when they are not. Smith therefore sought to discern social institutions that would reinforce imagination, sympathy, and a lively sense of being judged as if by an impartial spectator.

Smith was not a utopian. He had great trust in human experience and an experimental temper. He noted that district markets and fairs were, on the whole, happy places. Markets were very old institutions; it was not likely that they possessed no lessons important to social life. But the problem with existing markets, Smith observed, was that most of them were heavily regulated, to the benefit of producers. Businessmen seldom meet together, he observed, except in attempts to defraud the public, often by steering to their own profit the way in which market regulations are written and enforced. But this defect, he discerned, owed very little to principles inherent in markets as markets, and a great deal to the vulnerability of political regulation to manipulation.

Markets are ancient, but many of the ideas Smith contributed to understanding their potential are not. Neither Aristotle nor Aquinas observed that man has a natural inclination to truck and barter, as well as a natural desire to improve his condition and that of his family. But both these natural desires, first formulated by Adam Smith, by now have received ample empirical warrant.

Along with Montesquieu, Smith saw the pacifying and softening effects of markets on rude and savage behaviours. He observed that the essence of market activity lies in acts of mutual consent, indeed, in the common case, of mutual advantage. Markets appeal to human reason, and market dealings between two parties over time depend on mutual respect, trust, and sympathy. In this sense markets are civilizing institutions. Indeed, they lie at the heart of any practical conception of civil society.

On the dark side, no institution (not even the church) and no virtue (not even love) is incorruptible. Markets are also vulnerable to corruption and defects. Markets have limits; they are not an all-purpose tool; they do not accomplish all necessary social tasks; and they do not, even when they flourish, render

15

the state unnecessary. Markets are not a law unto themselves, but operate under both moral and civil law, as well as under many tacit codes and traditions understood by practitioners of each sort of market.

Thus, there are many things that ought never to be bought and sold; the truth, for example, or public office, objects consecrated to divine use, the human body (as in prostitution), etc. There are many human needs not well, or even at all, provided by markets, which civil society or the state have been assigned to meet, such as the welfare needs of those unable to function in markets (the sick, the handicapped, the old, the young), education, and certain public services. Adam Smith himself identified fifteen or sixteen such functions which the state or civil society would have to perform.

Nonetheless, markets kept as free as possible of unnecessary or positively harmful state-imposed burdens are instruments of the common good and civil society. Markets promote the swift transmission of economic intelligence, personal liberty, creative stimulation, enlarged sympathy and peaceable cooperation (even between strangers). They are a sign both of human interdependence and of civilized intercourse. The alternative to market exchange, freely and reasonably entered into for mutual benefit, is forced confiscation, command, or even war. To expand the reach and good working of markets, and to avoid their abridgement or misuse (e.g. by monopoly), is to serve imagination, sympathy, creativity, and liberty. It is also to place an open, dynamic, and other-regarding institution at the heart of the free and decent society. From the point of view of empirical sociology, as Peter Berger points out in *The Capitalist Revolution*,[13] no democratic society worthy of the name has yet been built on any other foundation.

As Muller shows, Adam Smith's 'civilizing project' entails a very large, capacious, and subtle understanding not only of 'the great system of public policy', with all the 'connections and dependencies of its several parts', but also of the philosophical vision of the 'commercial humanism' that it aims at. Simply to grasp this vision, let alone to pursue it, requires a certain public-spiritedness. For it is a social, systemic vision of ultimately planetary scope. It is history's first vision of universal economic and civilizational development. It is humankind's first practical and institutional glimpse of a world from which poverty will have been systematically abolished.

We are not there yet. We have a long way to go. We have much to do even in the 'developed' world before the 'civilizing project' is complete. Still, it must be noted that in the countries in which it has been tried, even fitfully and partially, the system Adam Smith encouraged his fellow humans to enter upon has more thoroughly—and, on balance, for the better—revolutionized the conditions of daily life than any other in history. Extremely poor countries of 1945, such as Japan, South Korea, Taiwan, and Hong Kong, have become rich countries by following this model, in their own way. (Their example shows that it is not true that the poor always get poorer.) By contrast, the Republics of China and North Korea, following other models, have remained shockingly poor. System matters. Social vision matters.

Empirically, by encouraging invention and enterprise, the market is the most remarkable social institution for the economic common good of humankind ever discovered, once set free to run strong in fruitful channels. The market was always available in human history, but its virtualities were never quite grasped in all their ramifications until relatively recent times, first of all here on this blessed Isle. I sometimes find it painful to contemplate how little these virtualities are still grasped, even here. Yet perhaps this is understandable. Before it exists as an empirical reality, the great system drawing together the centripetal liberties organised by the free market—like many arrows flying to one point—must be glimpsed and loved as a social vision. And why not? Socialism, despite its empirical failures, has always presented itself, first and foremost, as a vision. Why must the great combination of capitalism, democracy and pluralism—the true carrier of the dream of the free society—be denied vision? Curiously, the same people who think of socialism in visionary terms insist on confining the discussion of capitalism to its practical difficulties. The fact that capitalism, like all historical systems, contains ambiguities, does not prevent it from having an underlying moral vision—a vision of community, creativity, and liberty under the rule of law.

In fact, Adam Smith held that a passion for the public interest could only be excited if legislators, voters, and the young came to grasp political economy as a 'system'. They must love the idea and the principles of it, if they would keep it. He told his students:

> You will be more likely to persuade, if you describe the great system of public police which procures these advantages, if you explain the connections and dependencies of its several parts, their mutual subordination to one another, and their general subserviency to the happiness of the society; if you shew how this system might be introduced into your own country, what it is that hinders it from taking place there at present, how those obstructions might be removed, and all the several wheels of the machine of government be made to move with more harmony and smoothness, without grating upon one another, or mutually retarding one another's motions. It is scarce possible that a man should listen to a discourse of this kind, and not feel himself animated to some degree of public spirit.[14]

Not an appeal to excessive individualism, that. Rather, an appeal to public spiritedness, on behalf of a great, although limited and imperfect, social institution, whose virtualities the human race is still very far from plumbing.

In the next generation, I predict, the market will expand its liberating effects in Latin America, Eastern Europe, and Asia. It will also come to be used in new ways in the West, as an auxiliary device for making welfare systems work for the common good better than they do today. Markets will, I predict, excite civil society throughout the world with a new moral zest, and with imagination, sympathy, creativity, and regard for one another, under the rule of law. Indeed, markets will increasingly promote the gradual emergence of an international civil society. The state is likely to recede somewhat among international actors, while private connections among the world's citizens grow exponentially.

The vision of 'commercial humanism'—or 'democratic capitalism'—is international, not parochial; social, not individualist; realistic, not utopian; practical, not inflexible; open, not closed; and developmental, not static. It is human, and therefore ambiguous, imperfect, and flawed. It is subject to correction, and thrives best under vigourous criticism, even opposition. Go to it, then, as I conclude. The floor is open to questions and criticisms.

English Questions

Leeds University, June 1993

Question: *Is competition compatible with the New Testament?*

The Christian doctrine of sin practically demands that there be a division of power throughout the economy, such as the principle of competition effects. The alternative is monopoly, whether private or statist. In either case, too few acquire too much power. Given the propensity of humans to sin, it is better to have many employers rather than only one or a few, many producers and suppliers rather than a restricted number. Abuses are likely to be fewer when citizens have many alternatives.

For example, when there is only one major employer in a given district, prospective employees are at a great disadvantage in bargaining for better wages and conditions, etc. Their real choices are restricted.

When Hitler took power through elections in Germany, it was found that he could summon into one room all the major industrialists and financiers; there were too many cartels and too few rival power centres. Thus, the founders of the postwar 'social market economy' took pains to build into the new constitution a bias toward medium-sized and small firms, in order to diffuse economic power. That is a good example of the working of both human experience and a way of thinking influenced by the Christian doctrine of sin.

Question: *The mistake of capitalist thinking is to choose unrestricted liberty as its basic principle. Comment?*

'Unrestricted' by whom? There are sound reasons for minimizing the role of the State in abridging the freedom of conscience, and so we must distinguish arguments about liberty as a moral concept.

Humans alone of all creatures have the capacity to reflect and to choose, to be provident over their own lives, and in this sense they are made in the image of God. They have a unique responsibility for the choices they make. In this responsibility lies their dignity.

Morally considered, responsibility means choosing what we ought to choose, not what we wish to choose. Morally, liberty is always restricted by the full range of questions that a sense of responsibility brings into view. Conscience raises these questions. If our own conscience is weak (as in some areas it invariably is), others will raise these questions. Liberty is 'fettered' by these questions, you might say; or, better, is ennobled by the responsibilities they imply.

Morally, liberty acquires its sense of risk, danger, and excitement from such moral hazards. Politically, one might argue for the fewest possible further regulations or restrictions to be placed upon economic activities, and offer good reasons for this position. Contrariwise, one might base oneself upon a consideration of past experiences and argue that here, or there, further state regulation is needed, for these and those reasons. Settling such matters, about the degree of state regulation in particular cases, is a task for prudential reasoning, based on experiment and results, rather than a matter of principle. I know of no rule of thumb applicable in all circumstances.

Those who tilt in favour of the 'political' in political economy usually tend toward giving the benefit of the doubt to the State and its regulatory agencies. Those who tilt in favour of the economic side of political economy tend to give the benefit of the doubt to the private sector. Most on both sides probably agree that the burden of proof should be on government. The best proof is no doubt gleaned from experiment, either through lessons from the past or the hard way.

Question: Does not Christianity have an inherent link to the ideal of equality, and is not capitalism inherently unequal in its results?

Christianity teaches that only some are saved, others by their own choices damned, and that good servants may be distinguished from bad, foolish virgins from wise, and in short that moral and spiritual distinctions are to be made. Even the angels are said to be created by God in ascending hierarchies. Our God is not a God of uniformities, equality in that sense. You and I are not saints, and should not hold ourselves out as equal to them. Indeed, God's infinite perfection suggests infinite degrees of inequality. So it is simplistic to say that equality is a Christian ideal. In some senses, no; in others, yes.

Some nonbelieving philosophers have admitted that they borrow their humanistic ideal of compassion from the teaching of Jesus. They find nothing in the Greek or Roman sages, or in the practices of other cultures, quite like it. But since it is (as they think) human, they take it wherever they can get it. In this sense, we may as well speak of the christianizing of the pagan conscience as of the secularization of formerly Christian peoples.

Similarly, one will not find in Socrates, Plato, or Aristotle the teaching on equality among humans. On the contrary, they accepted the existence of slavery. Plato observed that relatively few men were 'of gold', only a small number 'of silver', and most 'of lead'. Inequality was the fact they stressed, not equality.

And again, Christianity (with Judaism) might be given the credit for stressing that all women and men are made in the image of God, and that therefore each is precious and has a fundamental and inalienable dignity, which even sin or fault does not take away. In this sort of dignity humans may be said to be equal, however widely divergent we may be in talent, gift, effort, virtue, achievement, concern, and luck. And Christianity (with Judaism) may be said to have brought this teaching into the world.

Notes

1 Maritain, J., *The Person and the Common Good*, New York: Charles Scribner's Sons, 1941.

2 Niebuhr, R., *Man's Nature and His Communities*, New York: Charles Scribner's Sons, 1965.

3 Novak, M. *Guns of Lattimer*, New York: Basic, 1978.

4 Hayek, F.A., *The Intellectuals and Socialism*, Studies in Social Theory, No. 1, California: Institute for Humane Studies, 1971.

5 Novak, M. *et. al.*, *The New Consensus on Family and Welfare*, Washington, DC: American Enterprise Institute, 1987.

6 Niebuhr, R., *Christian Realism and Political Problems*, New York: Charles Scribner's Sons, 1953.

7 Niebuhr, R., *Moral Man and Immoral Society*, New York: Charles Scribner's Sons, 1932.

8 Preston, R., *Religion and the Ambiguities of Capitalism*, London: SCM Press, 1991 and Cleveland Ohio: Pilgrim Press, 1993.

9 Taparelli d'Azeglio, L., *Saggio Teoretico Di Dritto Naturale Appoggiato Sul Fatto*, Palermo: 1840-43.

10 Pope Leo XIII, *Rerum Novarum*, 1891.

11 Johnson, P., *A History of the English People*, New York: Harper & Row, 1985.

12 Muller, J.Z., *Adam Smith in His Time and Ours: Designing the Decent Society*, New York: Free Press, 1992.

13 Berger, P., *The Capitalist Revolution*, New York: Basic, 1988.

14 Smith, A., *The Theory of Moral Sentiments*, Indianapolis: Liberty Classics, 1976, Part IV, chapter 1, slightly adapted from p. 307.

The Moral Order
of a Free Society

Ronald Preston

The question put to me is, 'How far does freedom rest on a moral tradition?', with two subsidiary themes; (1) 'How far does capitalism encourage selfishness?'; (2) 'What is the place of Christianity in western civilisation?'. Underlying the discussion, which is deliberately set in the context of the Christian faith, is a theology of civil society. However, the first two questions require us to discuss within such a theology of civil society the relation of Christian moral affirmations to those of other faiths and philosophies. It is clear that making moral distinctions is a characteristic of human beings as such; and that in the plural societies of the 'West', with which we are concerned, freedom must rest on a moral basis which is not exclusively Christian. And I take it that the free societies of our theme are 'Western' types of political democracies which stand for two things, majority rule and respect for minorities. The second is important because political democracy will not work if the majority feels it can ride roughshod over minorities (a point which the Protestants in Northern Ireland need to take on board more fully). Political democracy of this kind does not necessarily accompany a market economy, which is also a background to this discussion. The recent examples of Chile under Pinochet and the partial switch to a market economy in China indicate this. But political democracy is congenial to a market economy.

It is not necessary to dwell upon the place of Christianity in Western civilisation. With its heritage from Judaism and from the Greeks it has clearly been fundamental. Indeed of all the civilisations studied by Arnold Toynbee two generations ago, our Western one is the only one in which Christianity has powerfully woven itself into the social structures. That is why it has been meaningful to speak of Christendom in the past, and to refer to the present as a post-Christendom situation. For we have now been much affected by a secular humanist outlook, due to the vast technological and cultural changes since the Renaissance and the Enlightenment, together with a far more intimate contact with adherents of other traditional faiths. How does the Christian legacy relate to the political free, plural, market society of today? A brief historical survey is necessary to put this question in perspective.

Christianity, as its name implies, is centred in the ministry of Jesus Christ. In his teaching and actions the concept of the Kingdom, or Rule, of God is central. He lived what he taught; and his understanding of the nature of God's rule over his world was paradoxical in the extreme. God rules in righteousness not by punishing human wrong doing but by bearing the consequences of it himself. These consequences led Jesus to his death, seen by the earliest Christians not as a disaster but as a triumph. The Kingdom of God has far reaching ethical implications. Part of them are in line with the common moral insight of humankind, such as the Golden Rule, 'Always treat others as you would like them to treat you'.[1] However part go far beyond it, radicalizing love for one's neighbour, and requiring unlimited forgiveness of wrongdoers.[2] Indeed the more one learns of love as understood in the Christian faith the more far reaching and inexhaustible it becomes.

Civil society is not the focus of the Kingdom of God, it presupposes it. Caesar has his place and his claims.[3] The Kingdom remains a radical challenge, always searching for an expression in civil society, but never fulfilled in any particular expression, and always pointing forward. At first the expectation of the imminent return of Jesus (his *parousia*) obscured the problem of the relation of such a radical gospel to civil society, but as this expectation faded it soon became clear. Since then the problem for the church and for most Christians has been how to maintain this radical stance when there is no expectation of the imminent return of Jesus. It cannot be said that they have been very successful. The tendency has been to take a static view of established institutions and to sanctify them. This was more plausible when the speed of social change was slow. And that is why the advent of dynamic capitalist economies, with the rapid social changes that accompany them, was such a shock, a shock with which Christianity has been trying to come to terms ever since.

By the end of the first century of the Christian era the ethical teaching of the pseudo-Pauline Pastoral Epistles[4] had domesticated the radical Kingdom teaching of the gospels. Love has become one virtue among several, and the Household Codes are static and patriarchal. After the conversion of Constantine (whatever that was) the emphasis on the *status quo* became stronger. Radical ideas remained, but the tendency was to say that they belonged to the time before the Fall, and that the established order, particularly the State, was the remedy for the sins which were the result of the Fall. An hierarchical view of society, particularly stressing the duties of those low in the hierarchy to those above them, was characteristic. However this was at any rate a corporate view of society even though it was static. A market economy was to challenge both aspects. Positive social change, as we think of it, was not in mind. If anything the fear was of social decay, as evidenced by the rage and despair expressed by St. Jerome at the news of the fall of Rome. Later, Luther was to think it not far from the end of human history, and that the best that could be hoped for was that God would enable rulers to fend off the forces of disorder and decay. The 1662 Book of Common Prayer of the Church of England prays for the punishment by the rulers of wickedness and vice and the maintenance of true religion and virtue. It thanks God for creation and preservation. There is no thought of social change, or the remedy of social evils; an understanding of social justice plays no part in public worship. How could such a static and patriarchal social teaching cope with capitalism?

It had great difficulties. Traditional teaching on usury was the first challenge. The twists and turns of the discussion over three centuries are very illuminating. I have discussed them elsewhere and will not dwell on them now.[5] In the Roman Catholic Church traditional Moral Theology continued to be taught in seminaries and catholic universities, but in practice it was losing influence in social economic ethics until relaunched by Pope Leo XIII in his Encyclical *Rerum Novarum* in 1891. In Anglican and Puritan circles traditional social teaching, somewhat modified, continued for some time, but it collapsed at the end of the seventeenth century.

One of the causes and results of the collapse was the break away of various sciences from the medieval framework within which they had operated, in which Theology was the queen of sciences. Of the social sciences economics, or political economy as it was called, was the first to develop independently. England and Scotland led the way because capitalism developed first in Britain. A number of clergy were pioneers in this. Before the advent of specialised professions, a well educated clergyman had the possibility of advancing the frontiers of knowledge in many areas. Lacking any sense of a tradition of Christian social ethics, some of them argued on first principles against the prevailing mercantilist teaching in the eighteenth century. They said that God, as Christians understand him, could not have created a world in which one nation could only prosper at the expense of others. Mercantilism must be false. However, the next serious challenge came from a clergyman himself, Reverend Thomas Malthus. His theory of population was thought to be scientifically established, so that it could not be rejected on first principles.[6] But it was so dismal that a theodicy had to be worked out to justify the ways of God to humans, if the inequalities and miseries of the social order which it analyzed were indeed endemic. This task preoccupied several Christian thinkers in the first three decades of the nineteenth century.[7] The result was that a world of absolute scarcity, as Malthus led them to understand it, was to be administered according to the laws of competition in a free market. These laws were regarded as much a fixed element in the created world as were the laws of physics (as then understood). The social order which enshrined them was seen as divinely instituted for the moral discipline and training of sinful humanity. The very spontaneity of the laws of supply and demand warned against any attempt to modify them on behalf of, or by, the poor. It could not succeed. Since scientific evidence could develop outside the traditional theological framework, theology had to incorporate it into its account of God's rule of the world. It was a pioneering but flawed effort. The theology devised to deal with it was as flawed as the 'science'. Later the political economy in which it was expressed was to shed by the end of the nineteenth century the part theological and part philosophical trappings which had accompanied it, and economics as we know it to-day emerged. It is concerned with the *relative* scarcity of resources compared with the possible alternative uses of them; and with the market as an 'ideal' means of maximising the productivity of these relatively scarce resources, in so far as that is what humans want to do. In so far as humans put other values first, as to some extent they nearly always do, economics cannot prescribe their preferences; but it can tell them the probable economic cost of what they are doing.

To return to the situation around 1840. The theological post-Malthus justification of *laisser-faire* was dominant. At this point F.D. Maurice, one of the greatest nineteenth century theologians, returned to first principles and said that to regard competition as a law of the universe and as the basis of human relations is a lie. This basic insight heralded the Christian socialist movement, which dates from 1848. Beyond that insight Maurice did not go. He himself had not only an organic but an hierarchical view of society. He was not a socialist by any standard use of the term. The immediate so-called Christian socialist experiments were short lived. But later in the century, and in this century, various Christian socialist movements have developed, almost all acknowledging a debt to F.D. Maurice. In 1960 they all came together, some long standing groups, some relatively new, in one Christian Socialist Movement. It has produced several collections of papers and lectures, all but one of which I have appraised in review articles. The latest appeared in March 1993, *Reclaiming the Ground*, and it is on this that I now want to comment.[8]

However, at this point I need to insert a biographical paragraph. What happens in one's late adolescence is often very decisive for one's future attitudes. In my case, as an undergraduate at the London School of Economics, I was much influenced in three ways. The first way was by classical economic theory. All my teachers in economics were in that tradition and most of them politically could be called Gladstonian liberals. Through them I came to understand the market as an 'ideal' concept. Next, because I majored in modern economic history, I was much influenced, personally and intellectually, by R.H. Tawney, who was a Christian socialist. Indeed nearly all the teachers I came across in politics, history and sociology were on the left politically. Thirdly, I was one of the first in this country to read the acute social and political theology of Reinhold Niebuhr, often called Christian realism. Ever since then I have been trying to keep these three balls in the air, with varying emphases between them, and doubtless with varying success. It has put me on the political Left, but I have never been theologically happy with the theology of the various Christian socialist groups or with many of their criticisms of capitalism. Dealing with their latest book will, among other things, raise the question of capitalism's alleged encouragement of selfishness. After that I shall come to the moral order underpinning a free society, and the relation of Christianity to it.

The aim of *Reclaiming the Ground* is to re-unite the ethic of Christianity to democratic socialism. This alerts us at once. We have seen already that the ethic of Christianity is directly related to the Kingdom or Rule of God as taught and lived by Jesus, and that it bears witness to a radicalism which cannot be exhausted by any one social and political order. Indeed, John Vincent, in the one sharp theological chapter in the book, points out that the Kingdom of God bears witness to a radicalism beyond socialism, and at the same time points us towards the state of the poor as a prime concern.

We shall of course want to know what is meant by democratic socialism. The structures of it are not clear in this book, but I think it rightly stresses equality as a socialist concern. I shall return to this shortly.

The symposium makes a powerful criticism of the working of our present market economy in three respects. (1) The state of the poor; the Easterhouse estate in Glasgow being taken as an example. (2) The existence of a semi-permanent underclass; whilst at the same time refuting the contention of the New Right that it is the welfare state which has produced it. (3) The fact that the pure theory of the market ignores the community structures which underlie it. Many people, not only on the Left, will agree. The next question is this. Since we have good reasons to suppose that no economic system will be without flaws, and since capitalism has undoubtedly brought many benefits, what is a better alternative? Here the book is very general. Bob Holman refers to 'an insufficiently controlled capitalism'; Tony Blair to the need to get beyond a stale debate on state intervention versus *laisser-faire*; and Paul Boateng on wealth creation does not get beyond a reference to the inadequacy of an 'unregulated free market'. There is a passing reference to 'co-operation not competition', but John Smith says that governments must appeal to self interest. It is said that self-improvement must be combined with personal responsibility; and John Smith commends John Gray's conception of an 'enabling state' in a recent Institute Of Economic Affairs publication, *The Moral Foundations of Market Institutions*.[9]

None of this gets near policies and structures. Indeed two of the contributors, Bob Holman with a stress on local communities, and John Vincent writing on prophetic minorities with radical experiments, and on parabolic actions in alternative communities, seem to give up on questions of macro-economic policies and structures. In terms of ideals Tony Blair, with references to Tawney, stresses equality as the main concern of democratic socialism; equality is for the sake of proper relationships between human beings. He says this is central to Christianity. Beyond that he makes only the most general claims for Christianity, as far as social theology is concerned; that inherent in it are demands for personal and social change and hopes for a better world. Most Christians, apart from the most pietistic, would now agree with him as against the social pessimism so prevalent in Christendom in the past. It leads to a question not central to the present discussion but which is worth mentioning. In view of its radical origins in Jesus' life and teaching focused on the Kingdom of God, how is it that Christianity has been so socially conservative in practice, and how far should it be, if it be granted that Christians should not acquiesce in avoidable social evils? The justification would be if they could persuade themselves that any feasible alternative at a given time would be worse than the *status quo*. John Smith says that Christians need not be socialists, though he does not say why. Perhaps because some may well stress other values congenial to Christianity such as freedom. He also points out that those of other faiths may, and will, also be socialists. Blair, however, gives a hostage to Christian critics by saying that democratic socialism is based on a fundamentally optimistic view of human nature and, referring to Tawney, on a sense of the human potentiality of every man and woman. It is true that Tawney did stress the fundamental soundness of the judgements of the ordinary citizen, Henry Dubb (as he called him) as against the alleged moral superiority of intellectual and wealthy élites, but he was not starry eyed about humans in general, even though he was not as subtle in analysing the interplay of human vices and virtues as Reinhold Niebuhr. The latter was particularly effective in bringing out the insidious corruptions which prey on our virtues, much more serious than our obvious vices. Blair's blindness to this is characteristic of much Christian socialism. It enables those of the Right to score an unwarranted victory on those who understand the politics of imperfection, or Original Sin, to use a classic term. Indeed, as I have maintained elsewhere, arguments on the basis of human sin and irrationalism tell as much against the Right as the Left.[10]

This book is true to the main tradition of Christian socialism in that it shows no trace of being waylaid by the chimeras of Marxism, which betrayed many of the secular Left. Moreover it no longer makes much of the traditional Christian socialist criticisms of capitalism, chiefly three; (1) Competition in itself is ethically dubious; (2) So is profit; production should not be for profit but for use; (3) The motive for economic activity should be service, not self. I will refer to these in a moment. Secularly, the traditional nationalisation programme of the Labour Party has also disappeared from the book. Clause 4 of the Constitution might not exist. The strength of the book is in its stress on equality, and the need to criticise the ideology of individualism prevalent in capitalism. But *is* this a strength? Before assessing this I turn to those three traditional Christian socialist criticisms of capitalism, as a useful background to a consideration of equality.

Competition

I do not see any reason why Christians should be suspicious of competition as such. Both co-operation and competition are part of one's natural and spiritual growth, and discovering one's capabilities. There must be a division of labour in society, and that will mean some grading according to standards such as cost, quality, natural talent and acquired skills. That will mean there will be successes and failures in our human communities.

We all have to learn how to cope with successes and with failures. Our civic structures as well as voluntary associations should hinder the relatively successful despising or marginalising the relative failures.

Profit

There is no reason to reject profit as such, either as a motive for production or a directive as to what should be produced. Those who talked of production for use and not for profit did not understand the theory of the market, that it is the judgement of what goods and services consumers think to be useful that in principle secures that they will be provided, and profits made. No better way of deciding the allocation of relatively scarce resources in the present, and between present use and future consumption, is on offer. This however is subject to the social framework within which the market is scheduled to operate, of which more will be said later.

The Stress on Service Not Self

How far does capitalism encourage selfishness or, in the words of the ecumenical Oxford Conference of 1937, does it enhance acquisitiveness? It obviously tends to; but care is needed in thinking about this. First of all the self must be valued. Those who loathe or despise themselves are incapable of service to others. Concern for the self is not the same as selfishness. We must not ignore or underrate ourselves as unique persons. There is a proper place for egoism; we are to love our neighbours as ourselves. Indeed egoists can go a long way to what an altruist would approve, in seeing the wisdom of helping others to achieve their goals, in order to achieve a tolerable level of social order and stability, which is in their best interests in achieving their own goals. Even a distributive ethic on an egoist basis would be likely to stress need as a main criterion rather than desert, and for the same reason, though it would not be likely to be concerned with the disadvantaged beyond a fairly minimum level, unless they constituted a serious threat to the social order.[11] So I am well aware of the need to foster 'disinterested good will', and here the Christian churches have a major role to play. But society cannot be run on disinterested good will; it is too fitful.

A social order needs to achieve structures which foster the harmony of self interest with the common good. Or, as William Temple said, the art of government is to arrange affairs so that self interest prompts what justice demands.[12] Nevertheless, the structures of capitalism do very easily lead to greed and corruption. The pure theory of the market is an ideal construction. In reality there is much scope for twisting it whilst playing lip service to it, especially by the free rider who makes a buck by flouting what he hopes his rivals will stick to. Dealing with this is a matter of *political* economy and politics, not economics. And politics itself needs a built-in monitoring of structures against the abuses of combined political and economic power, and the corruption of selfishness to which it can give rise. The monstrous abuses of the combination of political and economic power in the collapsed Soviet style command economies are witness to this.

I come now to equality as the legitimate legacy of socialism, including Christian socialism. It is this which Tawney stressed, on behalf of an equality of respect, and for the sake of freedom and fellowship; not an equality of result, nor merely an equality of access, which by itself would lead to an unpleasant meritocracy. In my experience a stress on equality is often met with incredulity. It is asked whether one can be so naïve as to stress equality in the face of the obvious human inequalities. But at a fundamental level Christians must affirm it. Both as created in the image of God, and re-created to new life in Christ, Christians see human beings as equally precious in the sight of God, whatever differences there are between them in sex, colour, talent or character. The question is, 'How far should this fundamental equality be expressed in social policy and structures?' Differences between Christians arise here. Some take an otherworldly line. It has been argued, for instance, that the text of the funeral service is the same for rich and poor alike, and that this expresses their equality before God in time and for eternity. This evasion is less heard now than a century ago. Others stress the value of liberty as fundamental to the Christian life. Men and women must make their own decisions before God; no one else can live someone else's life for them. Collective processes must not undermine personal choices. As for fraternity both radical and socialist may stress it; the former its voluntary nature, the latter the need for corporate structures to foster fraternity. And those traditional hierarchies which have a sense of *noblesse oblige* bear witness to it in their own way.

However it is not only Christian socialists who stress equality. A powerful statement, and one which has influenced me, came from the humanist Walter Lippmann in 1927:

> There you are, sir, and there is your neighbour. You are better born than he, you are richer, or you are stronger. You are handsomer, nay you are better, wiser, kindlier, more likeable. You have given more to your fellow men and taken less than he. By any and every test of intelligence, of virtue, of usefulness you are demonstrably a better man than he, and yet—absurd as it seems—these differences do not matter, for the best part of him is untouchable and incomparable and unique and universal. Either you feel this or you do not ...[13]

If the role of the Christian socialists is to stress equality, leaving it to others to stress liberty, they can accept a central role for the free markets as the best device so far achieved by human beings to deal with basic economic problems which any society has to face. But they will be very conscious of its ideal character and the defects which in practice are inherent in it, and for which a political correction is needed. There are many collective needs it cannot meet, and disputes between Right and Left are likely to be about the extent of these. It also leads, particularly through inherited wealth, to great inequalities of purchasing power in the market. Resources are drawn to provide luxuries for some whilst the poor do not have the purchasing power to secure necessities. The assignment of productive resources seems more and more arbitrary. Therefore some redistribution of resources by state policy is required, the nature and extent of this being a standard content of political controversy. It is inequalities that need to be justified, particularly as to whether they do or do not work in favour of the disadvantaged, as Rawls argues in *A Theory of Justice*.[14]

I come now explicitly to the moral order of a free society. I agree with Michael Novak that democratic capitalism needs a moral theory about itself, a basic morality on which most citizens can be counted to agree. Any society must have some moral presuppositions to hold it together. The market economy needs to examine its moral presuppositions, for if it ignores them or fails to promote them, it is in danger of undermining itself. This struck me forcefully in visits to Hong Kong, an astonishingly successful economy in which nearly everyone seems engaged in making money all day and every day. It seemed to me it relied implicitly on the residual strength of the Confucian family ethic, which it did not attend to, and which if left to itself for many more decades it might undermine. Novak in all his social theology books writes eloquently of the positive moral features of a market economy, most recently in a booklet, *God and the Marketplace*.[15] He makes little use of the negative arguments of the New Right, that capitalism is the economic order for dealing with sin.

In this booklet, after some favourable comments on a recent book of mine,[16] he makes three criticisms of it. (1) That I ignore the democratic capitalist model of society as against the social market or democratic socialist models. But in fact the book criticises recent New Right advocates of the market economy as ethically unsatisfactory because of the individualistic ideology which usually goes with it. (2) I assume non-capitalist economies create less inequalities than capitalist ones. I make no such assumption; indeed I do not consider them because they are irrelevant to our situation, where some form of market economy is the only option available. (3) I do not refer to the ambiguities of socialism. But the critique I gave of traditional socialism does this; indeed one of the aims of the book is to stress the ambiguities (or trade-offs, to use a homely phrase), which any society encounters in balancing different values and policy considerations against one another. So I do not think, with respect to Novak, that these criticisms amount to much. My criticism of him is that he underplays the defects of the market and is not critical enough of the philosophy of individualism which has been associated with market economies.[17] Obviously to stress the importance of individual liberty and freedom of choice is to set a decisive value on each person. This can be on Christian grounds, as I have already mentioned, or on secular humanist grounds, such as that human beings are rational creatures, or that they are all of the same species, participating in one and the same reality. However, further reflection shows that the human beings who are to be seen as precious in themselves only truly became themselves in relation with others.

34

They need freedom *from* unnecessary restrictions, but also freedom *for* creative relationships with others; a properly human community.

Community is somewhat of a weasel word. It can refer to a society which stresses order and security rather than freedom, which is conservative and hierarchical. Or, at the other extreme, a society of equalitarian solidarity. It is a word in common use, and has other words in our vocabulary related to it; common, commune, communion, communication, communism. So it resonates in human experience. Christianity has indeed its distinctive origins, but its theology has roots in the common experience of human living; it develops this and deepens it. So it is with community. In Pauline theology the term *koinonia*, which we translate as communion or fellowship, refers to the deep relation men and women have in and with God and one another in the church, neatly expressed in the Grace, 'The Grace of our Lord Jesus Christ, and the love of God, and the communion of the Holy Spirit'.[18] So Christians have strong grounds for standing for freedom in the relationships between persons of equal ontological status as the foundation of social and civic life. And in a time when we are growingly conscious of moral and social diversity in a plural society, we need to seek some common ground for community in other faiths and philosophies, and promote it. I understand, for instance, that a Chinese character signifying person has also the thought of 'betweenness' associated with it. If so it is a heritage of a fifth of the world's population. It is also a sense of community which make family structures so important, where children can grow into responsible individuality in a community context. At the level of civil society a *koinonia* ethic should offer a basic security and significance to citizens, free from restrictions of colour or gender; it should encourage co-operative activities, and approach realistically institutional barriers in society, where a community ethic requires a better balance of power rooted in justice.

Some such understanding of persons as inter-dependent social beings can be spelled out in more detail. It illustrates how Christian theology can co-operate with all men and women of good will (to quote a phrase occurring in recent Papal social Encyclicals). One such is the Belgian theologian Louis Janssens:

The human person is (1) a subject (2) an embodied subject (3) part of the material world (4) inter-relational with other-persons (5) an independent social being (6) historical (7) equal but unique (8) called to know and worship God.[19]

All but the last could be agreed to by secular humanists. Kevin Kelly, who quotes this, adds, 'Whatever promotes or violates the good of the human person considered in this comprehensive way is respectively morally right or wrong. This is the basic criterion for a person centred morality'. The recent European Values survey suggests that in a less coherent and systematic way it is akin to what the majority of those canvassed would affirm.[20] The last seven of the Ten Commandments are a desiccated version of it. Also, in another field, an effort is being made to articulate a cross-cultural medical ethic, based on the four principles of respect for human autonomy, benevolence, non-maleficence, and justice as fairness.[21] There are good grounds for thinking that these are in fact implicit or explicit in the way the medical profession is trying to guide itself in the face of the explosion of issues in medical ethics in the last twenty to thirty years. It is all the more important to stress this because of some current attempts to allege the almost total absence of any common moral and ethical understanding in the post-modern world.[22]

I am not suggesting that all this is clear cut, but I am suggesting it needs to be thought through as the moral basis of a free society. It needs cultural institutions which foster human flourishing in these respects. Values will be held in tension. The freedom associated with democratic capitalism is too individualistic. The market left to itself without correctives also treats labour as a factor of production in the same impersonal way as it treats land and capital. We also need social structures which embody mutual giving and receiving between citizens, not leaving it to the arbitrariness of individual good will. This is what the welfare state is designed to achieve. In so far as it falls short it has lately been attacked for the wrong reasons. Freedom needs balancing by the stress on equality; but if this is taken too far it can become restrictive and inhibit the dynamism which has been the mark of capitalism. Adaptability, inventiveness, innovation, enterprise, curiosity are all much more stressed in modern dynamic societies than in the static societies of the past, including that of the New Testament. They have all bettered human life. And that betterment is needed by the two thirds of the world it has so far largely passed by. But moral depth is needed, or the new powers at our disposal will lead to disasters. However, humans also need stability and social security. Most of us fear dynamism if our personal interests are threatened. We need social structures which help us to adjust. The hopelessness of the underclass created by our Western market economies is a scandal.

Disagreements about particular policies will always persist, partly depending on which value is thought to need stressing at a particular time. Dynamism and security both need stressing. Both need to be maintained simultaneously. The best policy may not be some intermediate half way between them; it may incline at any one time sharply towards one or the other. My judgement is that in view of the strong individualistic theoretical and practical thrust in Britain in recent years it is time for a more corporate stress; and that we have something to learn from our West European and Scandinavian neighbours in this respect. Details of policy will always be problematic; but all parties relate their detailed proposals to some ideological framework, and it is this I have been discussing. It is the general direction, not the details of policy, with which I have been concerned. And I think it is the job of Christian theology to advance a critique of ideologies, whilst at the same time being self critical about its own.

Notes

1   Matthew 7.12.

2   Matthew 18.22.

3   Mark 12.17.

4   1 and 2 Timothy and Titus.

5   On usury see Appendix 1 'Usury and a Christian Ethic of Finance' in Preston, R.H., *Religion and the Ambiguities of Capitalism*, London: SCM Press, 1991 and Cleveland, Ohio: Pilgrim Press, 1993.

6   Malthus, Rev. T., *An Essay on the Principle of Population*, London: 1798.

7   On mercantilism and on Malthus see footnote 6, p. 161, *Religion and the Ambiguities of Capitalism*, note 5 supra.

8   (ed.) Bryant, C., *Reclaiming the Ground*, Spire, Hodder and Stoughton, 1993. Four out of the six chapters are Tawney lectures.

9   Gray, J., *The Moral Foundations of Market Institutions*, London: IEA Health and Welfare Unit, Choice in Welfare No. 10, 1992.

10 See 'The New Right: a Christian Critique' and 'The Politics of Imperfection and the Politics of Hope', chapters 4 and 8, Preston, R.H., *The Future of Christian Ethics*, SCM Press, 1987.

11 See 'Christianity and Self Interest' Hughes, G.J., chapter 4 in *Christians and the Future of Social Democracy*, (ed.) Taylor, M.H., California: G.W. & A. Hesketh, Ormskirk and Northridge, 1981; and Preston, R.H., 'Capitalism, Christianity and Democracy', chapter 1.

12 *Christianity and Social Order*, Penguin, 1942; re-issued by Shepheard-Walwyn & S.P.C.K., 1976, introduction by Preston, R.H., p. 65.

13 *Men of Destiny*, New York: Macmillan, 1922, p. 498, quoted in Jenkins, D.T., *Equality and Excellence*, SCM Press, 1961.

14 Rawls, J., *A Theory of Justice*, Open University Press, 1972.

15 Davies, J., (ed.), *et al.*, *God and the Marketplace*, London: IEA Health and Welfare Unit, Choice in Welfare No. 14, 1993.

16 *Religion and the Ambiguities of Capitalism*, 1991.

17 The latter criticism has to take account of *Hemisphere of Liberty*, Washington DC: American Enterprise Institute, 1992, in which Novak writes about community with some eloquence, but still in my judgement overplaying the market as an instrument of community by giving more space to the individual. He distinguishes himself from the New Right by identifying himself as a neoconservative, and describes himself as an adherent of the Catholic Whig Tradition, involving ordered liberty, person, community and enterprise. It is a novel reading of Tradition, but its merits for to-day will doubtless continue to be discussed.

18 2 Cor. 13.14; See *Changing Britain: Social Diversity and Moral Unity*, a Study for the Board for Social Responsibility of the Church of England, Church House Publishing, 1987.

19 See Kelly, K.T., *New Directions in Modern Theology: The Challenge of Being Human*, Geoffrey Chapman, 1992, p. 30; Janssens' article appeared in *Louvain Studies*, 1980.

20 For comments on the European Values Study see *Changing Britain: Social Diversity and Moral Unity*, 1987.

21 See the Symposium *Principles of Health Care Ethics*, (ed.) Gillon, R., John Wiley, 1993.

22 See MacIntyre, A.C., *After Virtue*, Duckworth, 1988, and the lively discussion it has provoked.

Other Health & Welfare Unit Publications

The Family: Is It Just Another Lifestyle Choice?, Jon Davies (Editor), Brigitte Berger and Allan Carlson £6.95, 120pp, 1993, ISBN: 0-255 36276-5

Three essays examine the consequences for individuals and for society of the breakdown of the traditional family. They argue that the family is not just another 'lifestyle choice', but vital to Western civilisation.

"The report says that society is paying a heavy price for the belief that the family is just another lifestyle choice." *The Times*

Equal Opportunities: A Feminist Fallacy, Caroline Quest (Editor), *et al.* £6.95, 111pp, June 1992, ISBN: 0-255 36272 2

"Laws banning sex discrimination and promoting equal pay at work damage the interests of women the Institute of Economic Affairs claims today."

The Daily Telegraph

"Let us not above all be politically correct. Let us not become overheated because the Institute of Economic Affairs has brought out a startling report entitled *Equal Opportunities: A Feminist Fallacy*." *The Times*

The Emerging British Underclass, Charles Murray, with Frank Field MP, Joan Brown, Alan Walker and Nicholas Deakin £5.95, 82pp, May 1990, ISBN: 0-255 36263 3

"Britain has a small but growing underclass of poor people cut off from the values of the rest of society and prone to violent, anti-social behaviour."

The Times

God and the Marketplace, Jon Davies (Editor), *et al.* £4.90, 145pp, 1993 **Essays by Rev. John Kennedy, Secretary, Division of Social Responsibility, Methodist Church; Bishop John Jukes, Roman Catholic Bishop of Strathearn; Professor Michael Novak, Professor Richard Roberts, Rev. Simon Robinson**

Is capitalism morally acceptable? Theologians representing the Roman Catholic, Anglican and Methodist traditions look at Christian thinking in the light of the collapse of socialism.

"various Christian theologians welcome the economic role of the market and endorse wealth creation as a primary good." *The Daily Telegraph*

Liberating Women ... From Modern Feminism, Caroline Quest (Ed), Norman Barry, Mary Kenny, Patricia Morgan, Joan Kennedy Taylor, Glenn Wilson £6.95, 101pp, 1994, ISBN 0-255 36353-2

Caroline Quest argues that 'power feminism' ends up having as little relevance to most women as the 'victim feminism' it is directed against. It is, she says, 'for pre-maternal young women' and 'is of little relevance and help to the realities of life for the majority of real women'.

"It would be a mistake ... to take anything but seriously the essay "Double income, no kids: the case for a family wage" by the sociologist Patricia Morgan."

Margot Norman, *The Times*

The Moral Foundations of Market Institutions, John Gray, with Chandran Kukathas, Patrick Minford and Raymond Plant, £7.95, 142pp, Feb 1992, ISBN: 0-255 36271-4

Distinguished Oxford philosopher, John Gray, examines the moral legitimacy of the market economy. While upholding the value of the market economy he insists on the importance of an 'enabling' welfare state.

"one of the most intelligent and sophisticated contributions to modern conservative philosophy."
The Times

"This powerful tract ... maps out a plausible middle ground for political debate."
Financial Times

The Spirit of Democratic Capitalism, Michael Novak, £12.95, 463pp, Feb 1991, ISBN: 0-8191-7823-3

"Michael Novak ... has done us a service in illuminating where the fault lines between right and left now lie." *Will Hutton, The Guardian*

"Mr Major ... might seek inspiration from *The Spirit of Democratic Capitalism* ... There is much to be gained from a skip through."

Joe Rogaly, Financial Times

Citizenship and Rights in Thatcher's Britain: Two Views, Norman Barry and Raymond Plant £3.95, 77pp, June 1990, ISBN: 0-255 36261-7

Two leading political theorists describe and discuss the rights and obligations of citizenship, Professor Plant arguing from a socialist standpoint and Professor Barry from a classical-liberal perspective.